The Heart's Deepest Truths

Poetry on Healing & Harmony

Samiksha Tembhurne

BookLeaf Publishing

India | USA | UK

Made with ❤ on the BookLeaf Publishing Platform
www.bookleafpub.in
www.bookleafpub.com

Dedication

*To my precious daughters,
Etiksha and Anshika,*

May these poems be your guide as you journey through life. In times of uncertainty, may they help you find the strength to face any challenge with grace. When life feels overwhelming, may these words lead you back to peace of mind and remind you that within you lies everything you need to rise above.

This is my wish for you: to always carry the quiet confidence that no matter what you encounter, you can find balance, embrace your inner calm, and trust the wisdom within you.

With all my love,
Samiksha

Preface

Life is full of challenges, uncertainties, and moments of doubt. But within each of us lies the ability to find peace, even in the most turbulent times. This collection of poems was written with that very idea in mind: to offer solace, clarity, and guidance to anyone who seeks it.

These poems are not just words on a page; they are a reflection of my journey, my thoughts, and the wisdom I have gathered along the way. I hope that, through these verses, you find comfort when you need it most, and a reminder that no matter the obstacles, peace of mind is always within reach.

As you read, I encourage you to connect with these words as if they were written for you—whether you are looking for strength to overcome difficulties, a moment of calm in a busy world, or simply the reassurance that you are not alone in your feelings. Life is a series of unfolding moments, and through these poems, I hope to guide you toward a place of quiet strength, where you can pause, reflect, and find inner peace.

May these words be a companion for you through both the quiet and challenging moments of life, offering comfort and wisdom whenever you need it.

Acknowledgements

I would like to express my deepest gratitude to my caring husband, Sandesh Tembhurne, and my loving father, VinodKumar Shende, whose unwavering support and encouragement have made this book a reality. Their belief in me, even during the most challenging times, has given me the strength to pursue my passion for writing and to share it with the world. Thank you for always inspiring me to follow my dreams and never giving up on my journey.

To my precious daughters, Etiksha and Anshika, who light up my world with their laughter and love. You may be too young to understand this now, but your presence has been my greatest source of inspiration. Your giggles, cuddles, and endless curiosity remind me every day of the beauty of life and the importance of perseverance.

This book is not just a reflection of my hard work, but a tribute to the love and joy you bring into my life. One day, I hope you'll look at these pages and know that every effort, every late night, and every word written was with you in my heart.

A heartfelt thank you to all my readers, whose kind words and encouragement have meant the world to me. Knowing that my writings resonate with you gives me the drive to continue sharing my heart through words. I am honored and grateful that you find my work relatable.

You can find my first ebook on Amazon Kindle.*It's just a click away* 10 Inspirational Poems to Change Your Life.

Thank you for your support!

1. Pause in the Noise

The world is running so fast,
That no one has time to think and reflect,
About oneself and others.

It doesn't take much to like, comment, and share,
But it takes everything to pause, think, and reflect.
But who has time for this?
No one.
All are running in the crowd of social media,
Where one feels more connected,
Where one feels more motivated,
Where one feels more inspired.
But the reality is opposite.
This crowd makes you alone,
Very alone,
Because this crowd doesn't have time to listen to you.

So better you take a pause, think, and reflect.
Time is yours, and
This life is yours.

2. The Mind Flows Like a River

The mind is like a river—
Anger, pain, love, joy,
All are objects of the mind.

These objects are like droplets of water that form the
river,
That shape the mind.

Meditating on these objects
Allows us to see the beauty of the river,
The beauty of the mind.
This brings calm to the mind,
And calm to you.

With this calm, you can control yourself and others,
Comfort yourself and others.

3. The Real World of Introspection

How long will you lie with yourself?
How long will you enjoy your fame?
Some moments of introspection will
Show you who to blame.

It's not the world outside that bothers you,
But the real world is introspection,
Where you see everything as true.

As I am, so they are,
Is the message you get.

Loving yourself and others
Is the only option left.

4. The Sea Within

Suffering is more mental than physical,
It all starts with a thought,
Which leads to numerous depressing thoughts.

Is it possible to stop that thought?
Thoughts are like waves,
Coming, going, then again coming.
But you might have observed,
That at one point, there is stillness too.
The sea is still.

How do we still the mind then?
That's the catch.

Work on your mind.
Practice meditation,
Reflect on yourself,
Question why it happened to you,
The reasons behind it.
Take ownership instead of complaining and blaming.

That's it,
And your mind is still,
Like the sea.

5. The Mind's Mastery

In the darkest night,
One dark thought passed by,

Making me feel dark inside out.
I looked at the moon,

But the moon looked back at me,
Telling me it's empty inside out.

This made me realize:
Nothing can help but our own mind.

Control your mind, or it will control you.
Control your mind with positive thoughts;
Otherwise, negative ones will dominate.

So I focused on myself with bright thoughts,
And positivity naturally followed.

6. The Doors of Perception

Emotions arise by association from labeled percepts,
Labeled percepts are due to your sense doors.

Of eyes—what you see,
Of ears—what you hear,

Of body—what you touch,
Of tongue—what you taste,

Of nose—what you smell,
These senses shape your truth as well.

Are you aware of your sense doors?
If not, confusion floods your shores.

You will have wrong views to hold,
And blame the world, so harsh and cold.

But look within, the fault is due,
Not to the world—but rather, you.

7. The Breaking of Relationships

Anger is inevitable.

It is natural to speak in anger.

But the breaking of relationships is not inevitable.

Why do people forget that differences are with thoughts,

not with people?

Thoughts are not static, and neither is anger.

But after anger subsides, hatred becomes static.

Relationships break,

Always,

Forever.

8. The Transformative Power of Love

When you feel love,
You give love.

When you feel hate,
You return hate.

Eventually, you realize
Hatred can only be ceased by love.

Reaching this understanding
Takes time—
Sometimes, an entire lifetime.

It's better to realize this
Before it consumes your life.

9. Love's True Essence

When I know that you are aware I love you,
Why should I force you to love me?

To love means to love—just love.
Like breathing,
Like a heartbeat.

To love means to set free,
And I set you free.

I love you so much that you are free to be free,
Free to be yourself,
To do as you wish,

Not necessarily to love me back.
Love isn't that.

10. Tears that Heal

The day was silent,
The night is silent,
I am silent.

The night won't pass
Until silence passes.
Silence will not pass as such.
The moon cannot help that much.
What to do is a question.

How the night will pass is a question.
The wounds of the heart are deep.
How to fix it is a question.

With wounds came tears, naturally.
Tears telling me to accept the reality as it is.
Tears telling me to accept my mistake, if any.
Tears telling me to heal myself, to be myself.

Accepting myself with all the good and the flaws.

Tears telling me that life goes on.
Tears fixed the wounds of the heart,
Giving me a new start.

11. Patriarchy

She said she wanted to fly.
He said he would let her fly.
She was soaring like a kite,
But he was holding the string.

12. Illusion of Proximity

I am under the illusion
That you are so close.
If that were true,
Then why aren't my secrets
Also yours?

13. The Remedy Within

The one who knows all is impermanent,
Yet suffers.
What's the remedy for that?

The one who knows hatred is ceased by love,
Yet hates.
What's the remedy for that?

The one who knows craving gives rise to suffering,
Yet craves.
What's the remedy for that?

What's the remedy in practice?

In practice, the remedy involves consistent and dedicated
effort.
It lies in developing wisdom, cultivating love and
compassion,
And addressing the roots of suffering.

It requires a commitment to self-exploration,
Self-reflection,
And the cultivation of mindfulness in everyday life.

14. The Path to Healing

You won't understand my words,
You have to feel me.

When you feel me,
Heal me.

When you feel me,
I am healed.
When you listen to me,
I am healed.
When you take my name,
I am healed.
When you have faith in me,
I am healed.

When you are happy,
I am healed.
When you are healthy,
I am healed.

Healing comes with you and me,
So heal yourself,
And I will be healed.

15. Beyond the Bloom

What do you see in a flower?
Just a blossom?
Or the color?
Or the petals?

I see much more.
I see
Clouds,
Rain,
Light,
Air,
Soil.
Without all these,
There is no flower.

What do I see in you?
Much more.

16. Seeing Things as They Are

Seeing things as they are,
And not as you are,
Will make you more happy and satisfied,
Because you will see the root cause of the problem.

Instead of taking the problems personally,
You will see that there is cause and effect for everything,
And you will realize that
How important it is to see things as they are,
And not as you are.

17. The Power of Silence

Silence can be conveyed through silence.
Why do you always need words to understand?
Words are powerful, I know.
But can you always speak words that are non-violent?

If not, then why don't you practice silence?
Love, anger, faith—all can be expressed through silence.
Practice silence.

18. Nurturing Growth

I sowed the seeds
With dreams of seeing
Beautiful leaves and flowers.
But neither did I see the leaves
Nor the flowers.
Why so?
Though I have watered them?

Seeds need water, light, and air.
Yet I kept worrying,
Thinking my part was done
By just watering.
How can seeds grow
Without all necessary conditions?

In life, your body may sweat,
Or your mind may toil excessively.
But don't worry like I did.
Don't cry,
Don't despair.

Analyze the other conditions
Needed for your growth.

Fulfill all the requirements,
And let yourself flourish,
Just as seeds grow
Into beautiful leaves and flowers.

19. Embrace Your Inner Lotus

Have you ever seen the radiance of a lotus become dull?
It's beautiful, even in the mud.
When you know you are confident and wise,
Beautiful and kind,
Why feel the need to prove it?
Stay calm like the lotus;
Your shine won't fade away,
Come what may.

20. Cultivating Right Views

Wrong views stem from a lack of wisdom,
And a lack of wisdom arises from ignorance.
Be mindful in everything:
In observing and thinking,
In analyzing and speaking.

21. The Power of Love

Just as ice melts in heat,
The heart melts when loved.

9 789369 543380